Operation Pangolin
Saving the World's Only Scaled Mammal

written and photographed by
Suzi Eszterhas

Ⓜ Millbrook Press / Minneapolis

This book is dedicated to Thai, for helping the
world fall in love with these incredible creatures.

Millbrook Press™
An imprint of Lerner Publishing Group, Inc.
241 First Avenue North
Minneapolis, MN 55401 USA

For reading levels and more information, look up this title at www.lernerbooks.com.

Additional image credits: mfto/DigitalVision Vectors/Getty Images (backgrounds); MIKKEL JUUL JENSEN/
Science Source, p. 11; Save Vietnam's Wildlife, pp. 17, 28 (bottom right), 29, 31, 34; Elisa Panjang, p. 35 (top
left); Jill Reznick, p. 26.

Maps on pages 13 and 15 by Laura K. Westlund.

Designed by Viet Chu.
Main body text set in Univers LT Std 45 Light.
Typeface provided by Adobe Systems.

Library of Congress Cataloging-in-Publication Data

Names: Eszterhas, Suzi, 1976– author.
Title: Operation pangolin : saving the world's only scaled mammal / Suzi Eszterhas.
Description: Minneapolis : Millbrook Press, [2023] | Includes bibliographical references and index. | Audience:
    Ages 8–12 | Audience: Grades 4–6 | Summary: "Pangolins are one of the most poached animals in the world.
    Yet scientists know very little about them. Discover how pangolin rescuers and researchers such as Thai
    Nguyen are working to protect these mysterious creatures." —Provided by publisher.
Identifiers: LCCN 2021052076 (print) | LCCN 2021052077 (ebook) | ISBN 9781728442952 (library binding) |
    ISBN 9781728462660 (ebook)
Subjects: LCSH: Pangolins—Juvenile literature.
Classification: LCC QL737.P5 E89 2023 (print) | LCC QL737.P5 (ebook) | DDC 599.3/1—dc23/eng/20211105

LC record available at https://lccn.loc.gov/2021052076
LC ebook record available at https://lccn.loc.gov/2021052077

Manufactured in the United States of America
1-50124-49809-4/22/2022

Contents

INTRODUCTION: MEET THAI

Thai has a special relationship with Lucky, one of his favorite pangolins at the Save Vietnam's Wildlife (SVW) rescue facility in Cuc Phuong National Park in Vietnam.

When Thai Van Nguyen was a young boy living in a small village in Vietnam, he watched local hunters capture a pangolin and its baby. Thai had never seen a pangolin before. He recalls, "It was really sad when I saw one baby pangolin with the mom. The mom put the baby on its belly and curled into a ball. But it could not protect itself and the baby from the poachers."

With tears streaming down his face, he went home. Thai told his parents that when he grew up, he wanted to save all the pangolins in the world. He studied hard in school and never lost sight of his dream. Now he runs the world's largest pangolin rescue operation and spends every day with the animals he loves.

Thai's incredible story and his dedication to saving pangolins inspired me to write this book. When I was a child, I had not even heard of a pangolin. I did not know anything about these enchanting animals. Most people know very little about pangolins. They are not aware that these creatures are disappearing and desperately need our help to avoid extinction.

As part of his work, Thai has introduced pangolins to people around the world and has inspired others to help save them. He has taught community members that there is nothing to fear about these scaled creatures and that pangolins have a lot to teach us about the wonders of nature and coexistence. "I think pangolins can show us how to live in harmony with each other and nature," he says. "In a forest, a pangolin keeps insect populations in balance. It does not destroy its forest home. In fact, the burrows a pangolin digs are even homes to other species."

Pangolins are naturally shy, and with their dropping numbers, it is rare to see them in the wild. But Thai and other pangolin lovers are working to save them.

"The first time I held a pangolin, I felt love and my heart was warm," says Thai.

WHAT IS A PANGOLIN?

Pangolins are bizarre-looking animals. People have described them as walking pine cones, artichokes with tails, and modern-day dinosaurs.

Pangolins are fascinating creatures. As Thai says, "There are so many things to love about the world's only scale-covered mammal." They are secretive and shy, which can be a challenge for the scientists studying them. Although scientists have learned a lot about pangolins, much about them remains a mystery.

Though they might look like reptiles, pangolins are the world's only scaled mammal. They live in grasslands and forests in Africa and Asia. Pangolins are some of the most vulnerable creatures in the world. Other animals can run from danger or use their claws or teeth to deter a predator, but a pangolin's only defense is to curl up into a tight ball so its tough scales protect its soft belly. The word *pangolin* comes from the Malay word *pengguling*—"one who rolls up."

Some people refer to pangolins as scaly anteaters because they eat mostly ants and termites. But pangolins are not related to anteaters. Their closest relatives are carnivores (meat eaters) such as polar bears, lions, and wolverines. Pangolins are insectivores—carnivores that eat insects.

There are eight different pangolin species. Some species of pangolins are nocturnal—awake at night. Others are only active during the day. They dig deep burrows in the ground or find hollow trees to sleep in. All species are solitary and mildly territorial. They mark their territories with urine, poop, and secretions from a special gland on their bottoms. These secretions smell a bit like the spray of a skunk.

When faced with a predator, such as a leopard, tiger, lion, or hyena, a pangolin rolls up into an armored ball. Its hard outer shell of scales protects its soft, unscaled face and belly from attacks. The scales overlap like the petals of an artichoke. Most predators can't break through those scales, even with their sharp teeth.

Scientists don't know how long pangolins can live in the wild, but the oldest one in captivity lived for more than twenty years. Scientists also aren't sure how pangolins pair up and mate or exactly how long the female carries a baby. Researchers are trying to discover the answers to all kinds of questions about pangolins.

ADAPTATIONS FOR ANTEATING

With its nose close to the ground, a pangolin can track ant trails to find its next meal.

Pangolins have many incredible and unique adaptations that help them survive in the wild. "One of the most amazing things about pangolins is how they are perfectly adapted to eat ants and live in their forest environment," Thai explains.

- As insect eaters, pangolins must protect their eyes, ears, and noses from painful ant bites. All animals can shut their eyes, but pangolins also have special muscles to close their ears and nostrils while feeding.

- Pangolins have poor eyesight. But they have an extraordinarily strong sense of smell. It helps them locate and track the insects they eat. Scientists also think pangolins may be able to detect predators by scent.

- Pangolins don't have teeth. Instead, they have long, sticky tongues that they use to lap up ants and other insects. When fully extended, a pangolin's tongue is up to about 16 inches (41 cm) long. That's longer than its entire body! In most species of pangolins, the tongue originates from deep in the chest cavity, from the last pair of ribs near the pelvis.

- Since pangolins don't have teeth, they can't chew their food. Instead, pangolins swallow sand and small stones to help them digest food. They have muscular stomachs with special spines, which move the stones they swallow to grind up the insects.

- Pangolins have large, curved claws that can strip bark off trees and logs. That's how they find ant nests. They also use their powerful claws for digging burrows and excavating ant and termite nests on the ground. When walking, pangolins keep their claws out of the way by curling them underneath their feet and balancing on their knuckles.

"When I watch pangolins eat ants, I am always amazed at how efficiently they can use their tongue," Thai says. "They can lap up many ants in one slurp!"

Pangolins have three claws on each foot. In addition to digging, pangolins use their claws to help them climb trees.

- Some species of pangolins have prehensile tails—the tail can grasp things, similar to an elephant's trunk. Tree-dwelling pangolins use their prehensile tails to hang onto tree branches. The tip of the tail contains a soft sensory pad that helps pangolins grip the branches.

- A pangolin's scales are made of keratin, a substance that is also in human fingernails. These scales overlap to provide a tough yet flexible armor for the pangolin.

Like many monkeys, some pangolin species can use their long tails to hold onto branches as they climb trees. A few species of pangolins have tails that are longer than their bodies.

Pangolin Anatomy

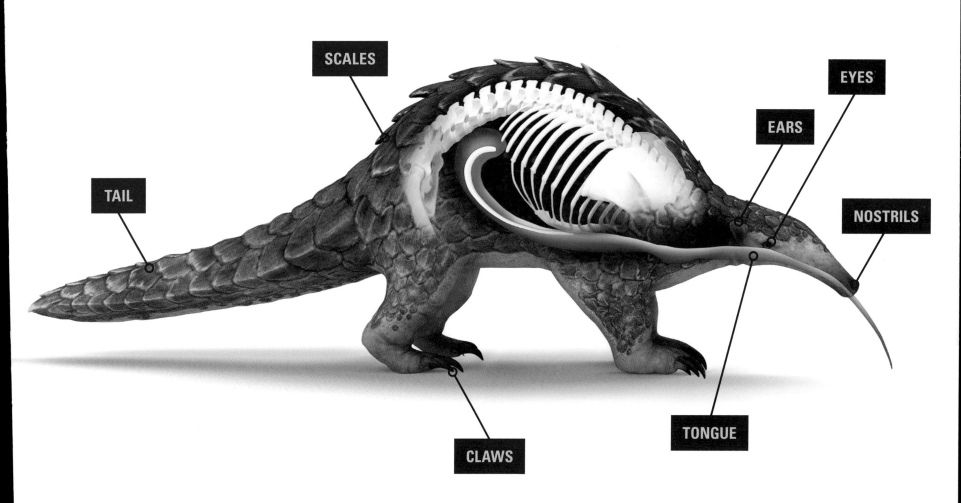

SCALES

EYES

EARS

TAIL

NOSTRILS

TONGUE

CLAWS

PANGOLINS AROUND THE WORLD

Of the eight different species of pangolins, four live in Asia. The other four live in Africa. Pangolins help keep ant and termite populations under control, which is important for the ecosystems in these areas.

ASIAN PANGOLINS

Chinese pangolins are found in more areas than just China. They live in southern Nepal, northern India, Bhutan, Bangladesh, Myanmar, northern Indochina,

Chinese pangolin

Sunda pangolin

southern China (including the island of Hainan, and most of Taiwan). They are nocturnal, and like other pangolins, Chinese pangolins are good swimmers.

Sunda pangolins live in Southeast Asia, from southern Myanmar to Laos, Thailand, Vietnam, and Cambodia, to Peninsular Malaysia, and to islands in Indonesia, Malaysia, and Brunei. Sunda pangolins live in forests, often near villages and towns. They spend much of their time in trees.

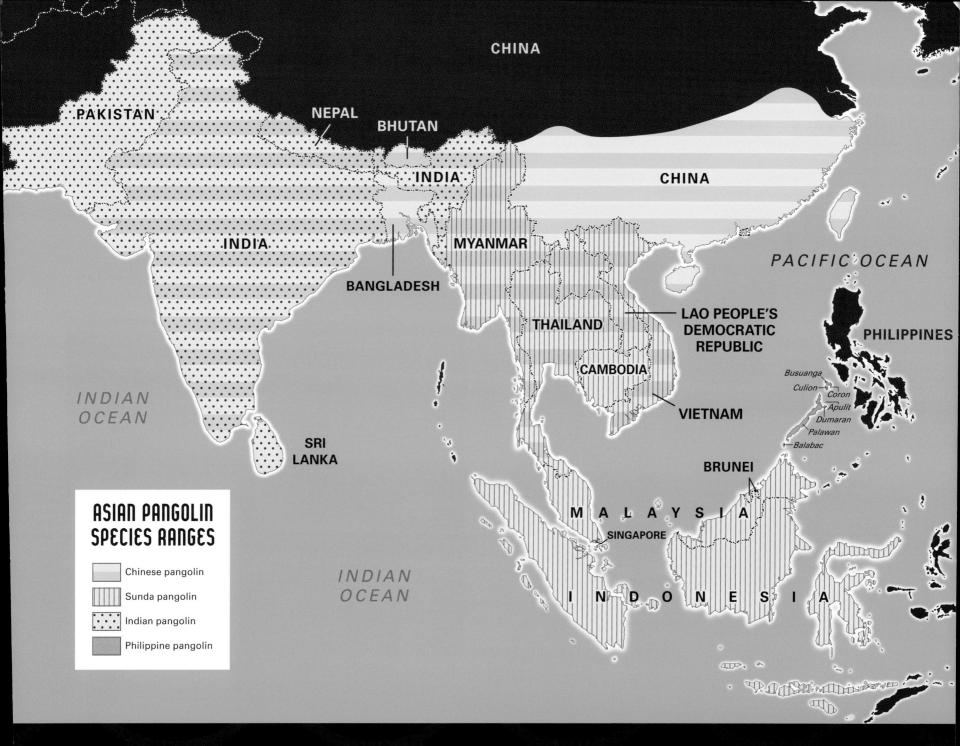

CHINA

PAKISTAN

NEPAL

BHUTAN

INDIA

CHINA

INDIA

MYANMAR

PACIFIC OCEAN

BANGLADESH

LAO PEOPLE'S
DEMOCRATIC
REPUBLIC

PHILIPPINES

THAILAND

INDIAN
OCEAN

CAMBODIA

Busuanga
Culion → Coron
Apulit
Dumaran
Palawan
Balabac

SRI
LANKA

VIETNAM

BRUNEI

MALAYSIA

SINGAPORE

INDIAN
OCEAN

INDONESIA

ASIAN PANGOLIN
SPECIES RANGES

Chinese pangolin

Sunda pangolin

Indian pangolin

Philippine pangolin

13

Palawan pangolins, also called Philippine pangolins, are found on only four islands in the Palawan Province of the Philippines. Scientists thought they were Sunda pangolins until 1998, when new information indicated that they were a separate species. Palawan pangolins have smaller scales and more rows of scales along their backs than Sunda pangolins have. Palawan pangolins often live in fig trees because the fruit attracts the pangolin's favorite food—you guessed it, ants!

Indian pangolins live all across India and surrounding areas, including Bangladesh, Pakistan, Nepal, and Sri Lanka. They can survive in a variety of habitats. Some even live in the Himalayan Mountains, as high up as 8,202 feet (2,500 m). Like all pangolins, Indian pangolins can adapt to live near people if plenty of ants and termites are available to eat.

AFRICAN PANGOLINS

White-bellied pangolins live in West Africa, central Africa, and as far south as northwestern Zambia and Angola. They were named after the white skin on the underside of their bodies. Their prehensile tails help them live in trees, but they can also be found on the ground.

Ground pangolins are the most widespread of the African species. These pangolins are found from northern South Africa through most of East Africa and into southern Sudan and southern Chad. They live entirely on the ground and prefer grassland habitats. They are mostly nocturnal, but in some regions, they may switch to being diurnal (active in the daytime) during certain times of the year.

Black-bellied pangolins can be found in western and central Africa, from Senegal, across the continent to Uganda, and south into Angola. They are the smallest pangolins. They have dark skin and scales, and have long tails. These pangolins are also diurnal and live entirely in the trees.

Ground pangolin

Giant pangolins are found in two separate populations along the equator of Africa. The biggest population lives in central Africa and a small part of East Africa. The other population lives in West Africa in coastal countries. Giant pangolins are the largest pangolins. They can be more than 4 feet (1.2 m) long!

All species of pangolins are endangered. But Thai and others are working to save them!

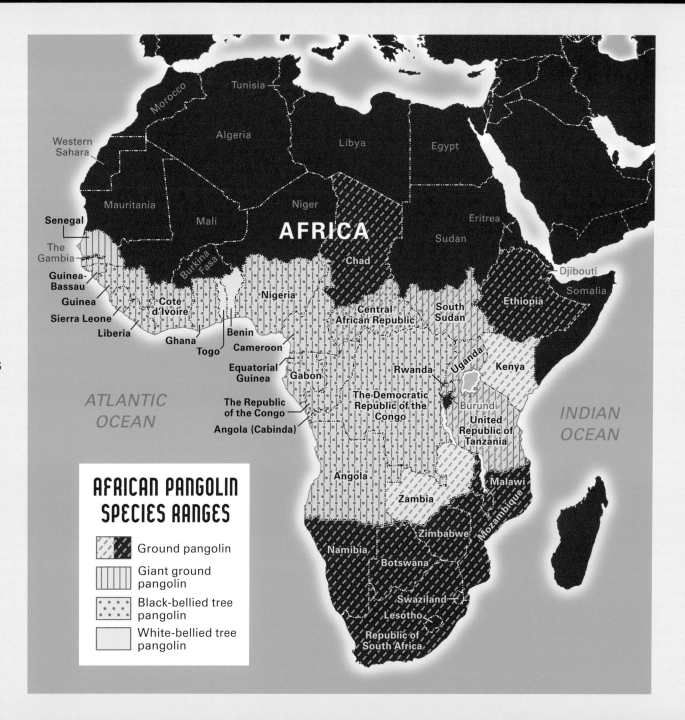

AFRICAN PANGOLIN SPECIES RANGES

- Ground pangolin
- Giant ground pangolin
- Black-bellied tree pangolin
- White-bellied tree pangolin

PANGOLINS IN TROUBLE

A pangolin's only defense against predators comes from their unique scales. But humans easily overpower these animals. "Humans are the reason why pangolin numbers are rapidly declining," says Thai. "If we don't act fast, we might lose them forever."

The armor that protects pangolins is also the reason they are in trouble. Humans hunt pangolins because some people in Africa and Asia use the scales in traditional medicine. For example, in Ghana, people use pangolin scales in rituals to cure rheumatism (swelling in the joints such as knuckles or knees). There is no scientific evidence to show that the practice works.

In China, Thailand, Cambodia, and Vietnam, some people eat pangolin meat. The meat is considered a delicacy—a rare and luxurious food often eaten by wealthy or powerful people. Some people in central Africa also eat pangolin meat. The meat is sometimes used in African and Asian traditional medicine as well.

It is illegal to hunt pangolins in most countries, but people still do it. This illegal hunting is called poaching.

Pangolin scales are worth a lot of money in illegal markets. A quantity weighing 2.2 pounds (1 kg) can sell for $1,000.

In some countries, restaurants have pangolin dishes on the menu. Pangolin meat is very expensive and prized, so people might buy it to impress their friends or business associates.

Every year, poachers capture about one hundred thousand pangolins from the wild. Conservationists estimate that poachers have killed more than one million pangolins in the last twenty years! Markets in some countries still offer expensive pangolin scales and meat for sale.

In 2020, the Chinese government increased its protection for Chinese pangolins to the highest level. China banned the consumption of pangolin meat and the use of pangolin scales in traditional medicine. Still, the actions of a single country, even a big country such as China, aren't enough to keep pangolins safe.

Thai explains, "If we are going to save pangolins, we need everyone around the world to work together. An individual, an organization, or even a country cannot do it alone."

Years ago, when Thai was growing up, people regularly saw pangolins in the forests of Vietnam. Now, wild pangolins are rare and rapidly disappearing throughout that country and the other regions they inhabit. "I don't ever want to live in a world without pangolins," he says.

In 2005, as a young man, Thai became a ranger at Cuc Phuong National Park in Vietnam. He rescued pangolins after poachers had illegally captured them and local police had then confiscated them from the poachers. These confiscated pangolins were often released directly back into the wild where they might not survive after the stress of being captured. Thai had to convince the authorities that he could help the pangolins, which were often malnourished or injured. It wasn't easy. Some police officers didn't trust that Thai would save them or succeed in caring for them.

At the time, no one knew how to rescue and care for pangolins. There was little research about pangolins and no instructions about how to help them. Thai had to learn what to do and how to do it. "There were so many unanswered questions," he remembers. "No one knew how to care for pangolins or even what to feed them."

Thai chose to rescue and care for an animal that scientists know very little about. It took courage and dedication, but Thai was determined to protect these unique creatures.

In the last ten to fifteen years, Vietnam has lost most of its native Sunda pangolins, making them rare in the wild. Thai's dream is to restore the pangolin population in Vietnam, so the species can thrive.

Over time, Thai managed to persuade many people that he could nurse pangolins back to health and release them safely back into the wild. After years of trial and error and reaching out to other pangolin researchers, Thai became the world's first expert pangolin rescuer. In 2014, he started his own organization called Save Vietnam's Wildlife (SVW). The nonprofit is dedicated to wildlife conservation in Vietnam.

PANGOLIN CHECKUP

When rescued pangolins arrive at SVW, they are usually exhausted, scared, thirsty, and sometimes injured or ill. Thai and his staff give each pangolin a physical exam. Pangolins are shy and don't like to be handled by humans, so Thai remains quiet and calm. "Many pangolins are very sick, hurt, and traumatized when they come to us," he says. "So I am careful to keep my movements slow and gentle. If I have to speak, I whisper."

Thai's team weighs the pangolins on arrival and once a week during their time at the center. Pangolins often suffer from intestinal issues while in captivity. Thai makes sure each pangolin is eating enough and maintaining a healthy weight.

Thai handles pangolins carefully during their checkups. This pangolin was only three months old when it was rescued from poachers.

During the exam, Thai feels the pangolin's body for any wounds or injuries; looks closely at its eyes, ears, and mouth; and listens to its heart and lungs with a stethoscope. Thai also weighs each pangolin, measures its body length, and takes pictures of each patient for identification. Then he takes its temperature and records its sex.

Since many poachers use wire snares to catch pangolins, the rescued animals often arrive with infected cuts or gashes from the wire. Thai and his team treat injured pangolins with antibiotics and clean their wounds each day.

Pangolins can carry diseases, so they must be monitored for three to four weeks at the center before they can be returned to the wild. Thai wants to make sure that sick pangolins don't carry diseases into healthy, wild populations when they are released.

Are you scared when you go to the doctor? You're not the only one. This pangolin rolled up into a ball to try to avoid a shot of antibiotics. These shots can help a pangolin fight off infections and keep it healthy.

HAPPY, HEALTHY PANGOLINS

Every pangolin is given water to drink and bathe in. In the summer, pangolins like to spend a lot of time bathing. Thai thinks the water might help them cool down or soothe ant bites. And in the winter, pangolins like to poop in water.

Pangolin enclosures must be made of concrete or stone so the pangolins can't dig their way out and escape. Thai adds natural objects, such as branches, logs, and tree stumps, so the pangolins can climb and remain active. Sometimes, Thai hides ant nests inside

Pangolins in captivity need something to do while they recover. Climbing on branches in their enclosures is an excellent activity.

Pangolins are sensitive and very difficult to care for in captivity. A good pangolin home must be warm, quiet, and free of stress. Thai works hard to make rescued pangolins feel cozy in their temporary shelters. At SVW, he prepares a special enclosure for each pangolin, which includes a den box (an artificial burrow) with leaf litter or straw for bedding.

Nutritious food is essential in keeping a pangolin comfortable and healthy. Of course, ants are always on the menu. A single pangolin in the wild can consume up to twenty thousand ants in a day! Where does Thai find all those ants? He uses a combination of wild harvested ants and farmed ants. To make his job easier, he also created a special recipe of frozen whole ants and powdered silkworm pupae.

When pangolins find food, they might stand on their back legs so they can use their front feet to dig into a tasty ant nest.

Rescued pangolins eat mostly frozen ants, but sometimes the pangolins get a live ant nest as a special treat.

the logs—pangolins like to search for their favorite food! These activities keep their muscles strong and give the pangolins something to do. Bored pangolins can become sad or stressed in captivity, so enrichment activities are important in keeping them healthy. "A pangolin recovering from trauma, illness, or injury will not survive if they are not happy," Thai explains.

A TINY SURPRISE

One day while he was checking on a female pangolin at SVW, Thai was surprised to find a tiny, pink newborn baby nestled up with its mom! It's very difficult to tell when a pangolin is pregnant, especially when it is not monitored for the entire pregnancy. A female pangolin does gain weight while pregnant, but the change is not always noticeable with rescued pangolins. That's because they often gain weight while in Thai's care after their poor treatment from poachers.

A mother pangolin can give birth to up to three babies at a time.

A pangolin mother protectively rolls around her pup in a den. Pups stay with their moms for about six months, depending on the species.

Nobody in the organization was expecting the baby. "We couldn't believe it! One morning when we checked her den box we found a tiny baby pangolin," Thai recalls. He and his team were extra careful to be quiet and let the mom and baby get the rest they needed.

A baby pangolin is called a pup. In the wild, pups are born in the darkness of an underground burrow or a hollow log. They are born pink and already have all their scales, up to one thousand! At birth, their scales are soft, but they harden within a few days. The mother leaves her pup tucked away in her den while she goes out to forage for ants. She returns often to feed the milk she produces to the pup.

A baby pangolin has to hold on tight as its mother climbs over tree roots and digs for food. The pup securely hooks its claws onto its mom's scales so it won't fall off.

When the pup is about a month old, it begins riding on the mother's tail during foraging trips. This is a chance for the pup to learn about the world outside the den and taste ants for the first time. The pup will continue to drink its mother's milk for another three months. After that, it will eat only ants, termites, and other insects.

A pangolin pup doesn't often leave the den during the first few months of life, while it is fragile and small. Leaving the den is also a risk because the mom might abandon the baby if she becomes too stressed. So after the surprise baby pangolin was born, Thai knew he'd have to keep the mother and baby at SVW for a few months. Soon the pup would be strong enough to be released with its mom in the wild. Meanwhile, Thai made their enclosure extra comfortable with lots of soft bedding and kept the temperature warm.

As a pangolin pup grows stronger and more adventurous, it begins to leave its mom's back for brief periods to forage for ants.

A caretaker carefully places a pangolin into a transport box so it can be moved to a safe location to be released.

Thai rescues and cares for many pangolins. His goal is to release them back into the wild. Every pangolin is different, but most adult pangolins stay with Thai at SVW for three to four weeks. Pangolins are released into the wild when they are fully recovered from any injuries or illnesses.

Thai plans and prepares carefully for the release of any pangolin. He must find a safe place where the pangolin will have enough food to eat and can avoid poachers. Thai and his team choose government-protected forests with lots of ant nests and water sources.

When the pangolins are ready for release into the wild, the SVW team puts them into transport boxes. Each pangolin has soft bedding, food, and water for the journey. The team members carry the pangolins to safe locations, which can be many miles away. They

The forest is the best place for a pangolin, but the transition from rescue to the wild can be stressful. Before release, Thai must be certain that each pangolin is healthy and strong enough to survive in the wild.

Thai says, "For each and every pangolin that we release back into the wild, I breathe a sigh of relief. I know they are safe and where they belong."

travel by road, motorbike, or even on foot. Gently and quietly, the team sets the transport box down and opens the door. When the pangolin feels safe, it will crawl out of the box and enter its new forest home.

"The most wonderful moment is when we watch the rescued pangolins slowly walk into the forest, because the forest is their true home," Thai says.

Though Thai worries about the pangolins, he monitors them after their release into the wild. Nearly 85 percent of them survive. This makes Thai's release program one of the most successful of all wildlife rehabilitation programs!

Thai teaches local children that pangolins might look scary or different, but they are not dangerous to humans. They have an important job in keeping the ecosystem healthy—they control nature's pests. One pangolin can eat seventy-three million ants in one year. That's quite an impact!

Thai knows that the key to saving pangolins is to stop them from being hunted. He must correct people's misguided or inaccurate beliefs about pangolins. Though many people believe pangolin scales have medicinal powers, there is no scientific evidence that they do. Thai and his team members teach people the truth about pangolins. They do not have medicinal value, but they are special living creatures that are important to Vietnam's ecosystems.

"I want the Vietnamese to be proud of their wildlife," explains Thai. "Our country has some of the most beautiful, unique species of animals that can be found nowhere else in the world."

These students share their love of pangolins at the Carnivore and Pangolin Education Centre.

Thai also works with police and legal authorities to develop stronger laws and better enforcement to protect pangolins from poachers. Thai helps train police officers, rangers, and customs officers how to identify pangolins and other animals that might have been poached.

As a wildlife conservationist, Thai is passionate about helping other endangered species that live alongside pangolins in the forests of Vietnam. His team helps save animals such as this endangered Owston's civet.

Most children in Vietnam don't get the chance to learn about wild animals in school. Many of them fear pangolins and other wildlife. In 2016, Thai and his team at SVW built the Carnivore and Pangolin Education Centre. Here, they teach children and community members about pangolins, why they are important to Vietnam's forests, and what people can do to protect them. SVW trains rangers and animal keepers as well.

Thai and his team at SVW are not the only people who have been working to protect pangolins. Thai works closely with zoos around the world because they also play an important role in pangolin conservation. At zoos, people can learn about pangolins and the threats they face. Some zoos help raise funds for Thai and other pangolin conservation organizations.

Since pangolins are sensitive and often die in captivity from intestinal problems, zoo workers had to

Each new pangolin at the Taipei Zoo offers an opportunity to learn more about pangolin behavior. That helps guide new conservation efforts to save pangolins in the wild.

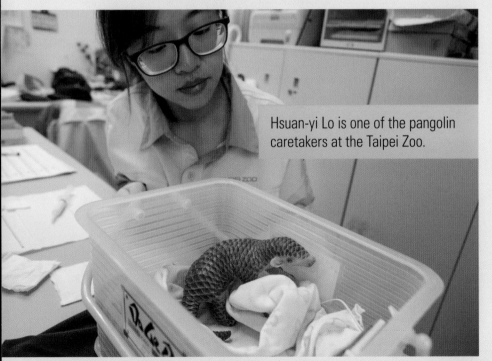

Hsuan-yi Lo is one of the pangolin caretakers at the Taipei Zoo.

figure out how to care for captive pangolins, just as Thai did. The Taipei Zoo in Taiwan has cared for pangolins for over thirty years. The zoo's animal behaviorists and scientists invented the pangolin cake. The nutritious pangolin food is made of bee pupae, mealworms, apples, eggs, calcium carbonate, yeast, and coconut.

The Taipei Zoo also breeds pangolins. For critically endangered species, such as the Chinese pangolin, a breeding program can help safeguard the future of the species. Hsuan-yi Lo, a research assistant at the Taipei Zoo, is a "pangolin nanny." She cares for newborn pangolin pups that cannot live with their mothers. One such pangolin pup, Gung-wu, was born to a mother rescued from poachers. Gung-wu was not able to latch on to her mother's teat to nurse, so Lo became her nanny. Lo spent months feeding, cleaning, and caring for her. Because of Lo's loving attention and a lot of hard work, Gung-wu survived. She grew up and had her own pups.

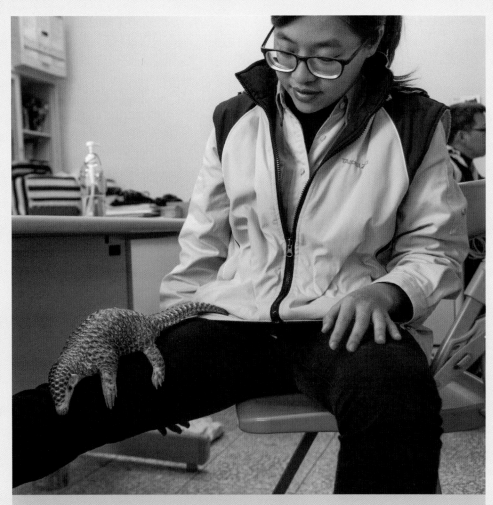

When Gung-wu grew older, she enjoyed clinging to Lo's leg, the same way a baby pangolin would cling to its mom's tail.

At only twelve days old, Gung-wu fit into the palm of Lo's hand.

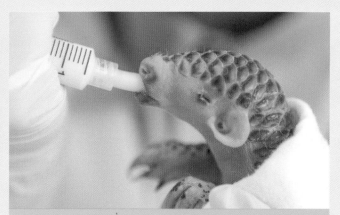

Being a pangolin nanny is hard work! In the beginning, Lo had to feed Gung-wu every hour, so Lo experienced many sleepless nights.

SOLVING PANGOLIN MYSTERIES

Saving a species humans know little about is difficult. Pangolin scientists work hard to find their shy subjects, often in the dark of night, and then carefully study and observe pangolins to better understand these mysterious animals.

Thai is a pangolin rescuer, but he is also a researcher. He monitors his rescued pangolins after their release. He uses camera traps, radio tags, and drones to learn about pangolins' movements, home ranges, and survival rates. Thai also searches for new habitats that might be safe and suitable for pangolins. "We need to know that the forests that we release our pangolins into are safe from poaching and logging," he explains.

Elisa Panjang studies Sunda pangolins on the island of Borneo in Malaysia. Like Thai, she fell in love with pangolins as a small child and has been passionate about them ever since. She investigates what happens to pangolins when their forest habitats are chopped down. Elisa educates local children about pangolin conservation as well. She also works to strengthen laws that protect pangolins in Malaysia.

Thai places camera traps close to the ground so he can capture pictures of pangolins searching for food in the forest.

With the help of radio telemetry, Elise Panjang can follow and track pangolins for long periods, even years. The antenna picks up signals from small transmitters attached to wild pangolins.

The transmitter on this ground pangolin's back helps Wendy Panaino find it in the Kalahari Desert. These devices are harmless to the animals and allow researchers to keep track of a pangolin's movements.

Wendy Panaino studies ground pangolins in the Kalahari Desert in South Africa. She is especially interested in how rising temperatures caused by climate change might affect pangolins. Wendy uses radio telemetry to follow wild pangolins and learn their habits. As she follows the creatures, Wendy collects scat, or poop, which can tell her what the pangolins are eating. She also sets up camera traps to photograph pangolins and other wildlife that cross the camera's motion-sensing laser beam.

PANGOLINS NEED YOUR HELP

Pangolins need help from humans to survive. Regardless of where you live in the world, there are multiple ways you can help pangolins.

- Become a species ambassador for pangolins. Learn as much as you can about them, and tell your friends and family what you love most about pangolins. People should know that these animals exist and that they need our help. You can even start a club and encourage your friends to join your efforts.

- Get artsy! Share your love of pangolins by drawing, painting, or sculpting them. Or write poetry or original stories about them. Then share with your classmates, family, and friends.

- Hold your own fundraiser to raise money for pangolins, and then donate the money to the Pangolin Crisis Fund. It helps fund pangolin organizations such as Thai's SVW. Here are some awesome kids who have raised funds for pangolins in creative ways:

  » Allie and her mom held bake sales and raised more than $1,500 for pangolins.

  » Ryan dressed up like a pangolin for Halloween. Instead of asking for candy when he went trick-or-treating, he asked for donations to help pangolins. He continued his fundraising after Halloween and raised more than $1000!

  » Landon made his own holiday ornaments and sold them. He told each of his customers about the threats that pangolins face. This introduced one thousand new people to pangolin conservation!

- Celebrate pangolins on World Pangolin Day, the third Saturday of February every year. Have a pangolin party with your friends where you make pangolin art or dress up like pangolins.

- Of course, don't eat pangolin meat and don't buy any real pangolin products.

Glossary

anatomy: the physical structure of an organism or any of its body parts

antibiotic: a substance that treats or prevents infections by killing or limiting the growth of bacteria

captivity: held or contained in a way that prevents escape

carnivore: an animal that feeds on meat

conservationist: a person who supports conservation including the protection of natural resources such as forests and the protection of wildlife and their habitats

diurnal: active during the day

ecosystem: a community made up of all the living organisms in a place, interacting with one another and with their environment

endangered: a species facing a high risk of extinction

excavate: to hollow out; to form a hole in

extinct: a species that no longer has any living members

habitat: the place or type of environment where a living thing naturally lives or grows

insectivore: a type of carnivore that feeds on insects

intestinal: relating to the intestines

mammal: a warm-blooded animal with a backbone that feeds its young with milk produced by the mother and has skin usually more or less covered with hair

medicinal: something used to cure a disease or relieve pain

monitor: to watch, observe, or look after

nocturnal: active at night

poaching: to hunt or fish unlawfully

predator: an animal that survives by killing and eating other animals

prehensile: capable of grasping especially by wrapping around

radio telemetry: a technique that uses radio signals sent from an attached or implanted transmitter to help researchers locate an animal

reptile: any of a group of cold-blooded, air-breathing vertebrates (such as snakes, lizards, turtles, and alligators) that usually lay eggs and have skin covered with scales or bony plates

sensitive: easily or strongly affected or hurt

solitary: growing or living alone

species: a category of living things that is made up of related living things that have similar traits and are able to produce offspring together

species ambassador: a person who helps educate others about a species of animal, the types of threats they face, and what others can do to help

stress: a physical, chemical, or emotional factor that causes bodily or mental tension

territory: an area that is occupied and defended by an animal or group of animals

transmitter: a device that sends radio or television signals to another device

Further Reading and Websites

Books

Duling, Kaitlyn. *Vietnam*. New York: Cavendish Square, 2019.
Take an in-depth look at Vietnam in this book, which covers its environment, geography, history, economy, food, traditions, and more.

Hansen, Grace. *Pangolin*. Minneapolis: Abdo Kids Jumble, 2021.
Read more about pangolins living in Asia. View full-color photos, and learn fun facts.

Schildwachter, Lori. *The Pangolin Revelation*. Mt. Pleasant, SC: Arbordale, 2021.
Discover other animals with similar adaptations to pangolins in this charming story of a boy who creates a new animal for a school project.

Websites

Pangolin Crisis Fund
https://www.pangolincrisisfund.org/
Find out more about the organizations that work to save pangolins around the world and how you can help them.

Pangolin Facts
https://kids.nationalgeographic.com/animals/mammals/facts/pangolin
The *National Geographic Kids* site has fun facts and photos of pangolins.

Save Vietnam's Wildlife
https://svw.vn/
Learn more about the organization Thai Van Nguyen founded, including information about the animals they save, their outreach programs, and their current efforts to combat poaching and protect wildlife.

Index